# LIVE

## In God's World

## The Word Is Life

Rev. Gerard P. Weber
Rev. James J. Killgallon
Sr. M. Michael O'Shaughnessy, O.P.

**Benziger**
A division of Benziger Bruce & Glencoe, Inc.
Encino, California

*Additional Photography:*
Steve McBrady
Cyril A. Reilly
Whit Collins

*Additional Graphics:*
THE WORKS, Studio City, California
Design: Clewer/Cook/Perez
Wire Sculptures: S. Anson
Illustrations: J. Perez, S. Nethery

Nihil Obstat:
   Robert R. Monahan, O.F.M.
   Censor Deputatus

Imprimatur:
   †William Cardinal Baum
   Archbishop of Washington
   December 6, 1976

Nihil Obstat:
   Austin B. Vaughan, S.T.D.

Imprimatur:
   †James P. Mahoncy, D.D.
   Vicar General
   Archdiocese of New York
   September 13, 1972

The nihil obstat and imprimatur are official declarations that a book or pamphlet is free of doctrinal or moral error. No implication is contained therein that those who have granted the nihil obstat and imprimatur agree with the contents, opinions or statements expressed.

Copyright © 1977, 1973 by Benziger Bruce & Glencoe, Inc. All rights reserved. No part of this book may be reproduced or transmitted in any form or by any means, electronic or mechanical, including photocopying, recording, or by any information storage and retrieval system, without permission in writing from the Publisher.

Benziger
A division of Benziger Bruce & Glencoe, Inc.
17337 Ventura Boulevard
Encino, California 91316
Collier Macmillan Canada, Ltd.

Printed in the United States of America.

# Contents

## Jesus Loves People — 2
1. Let Us Learn about Jesus ................. 4
2. Jesus Wants Children to Be Happy ........ 6
3. Jesus Wants Grown-Ups to Be Happy ..... 8
4. Jesus Wants All People to Be Happy ..... 10
5. Review ................................. 12

## Our World Is Wonderful — 14
6. We Love Flowers ....................... 16
7. We Love Animals ....................... 18
8. We Need Water to Live and Be Happy .... 20
9. We Care for the Things Around Us ...... 22
10. Cities and Towns Are Wonderful ........ 24
11. We Enjoy the Country .................. 26
12. We Enjoy the World God Gives Us ....... 28
13. Review ................................ 30

## Jesus Helps People — 32
14. Jesus Helps Sick People ................ 34
15. Jesus Helps People at Work ............. 36
16. Jesus Helps People Who Are Afraid ...... 38
17. Jesus Helps Hungry People .............. 40
18. Jesus Tells Us to Help People .......... 42
19. Review ................................ 44

## Jesus Teaches Us About His Family — 46

20. Jesus Tells Us That God Is His Father ..... 48
21. Jesus Tells Us That God Our Father Always Loves Us ..... 50
22. We Are All Members of God's Family ..... 52
23. Jesus Helps His Brothers and Sisters Today ..... 54
24. The Family of God Gathers at Mass ..... 56
25. Jesus Is with Us ..... 58
26. Review ..... 60

## The Life of Jesus — 62

Mary is God's Mother and Our Mother, Too ..... 64
The First Christmas ..... 70
Jesus Grows Up ..... 72
Jesus Cares for People ..... 74
A Big Party ..... 76
Jesus Told Stories ..... 78
Jesus Has a Special Meal ..... 80
Jesus Gives His Life for His Friends ..... 82
Jesus Is With Us ..... 84
Prayers ..... 90

LIVE

# 1. Jesus Loves People

# Let Us Learn about Jesus

We all like to learn new things.
This year we will learn numbers,
and letters, and drawing.
This year, we will also learn
about Jesus.

# Jesus Wants Children to Be Happy

Jesus wants all children
   to be happy.
He wants children to laugh,
   and to play,
   and to talk to each other.

# Jesus Wants Grown-Ups to Be Happy

Jesus wants grown-ups to be happy.
He helps them to work and play,
to love and care
for their families.

# Jesus Wants All People to Be Happy

Jesus wants all people
   to be happy together.
He wants children and grown-ups
   to help each other.
He wants them to learn
   from each other.

# 2. Our World Is Wonderful

# We Love Flowers

We love flowers.
Jesus loves flowers.
Jesus said,
"Look at the flowers
on the hill.
See how they grow.
See how nice they are!"

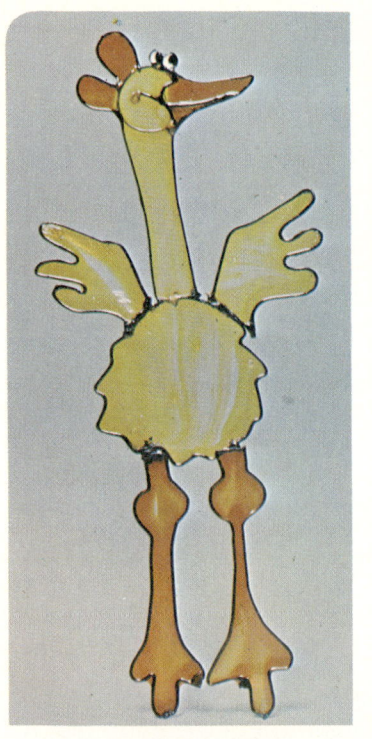

# We Love Animals

We love animals.
Jesus loves animals.
Jesus said,
   "Look at the birds in the sky.
   See how they fly
      through the air.
   Hear them sing.
   How wonderful they are!"

# We Need Water to Live and Be Happy

Everybody likes water.
We can swim in water.
It cools us in the warm weather.
It takes away our thirst.
Jesus knows that we need water
    to be well and happy.

But there are things that
    we must know about water.
We must keep it clean.
We should not throw things into
    the lakes,
    and streams,
    and rivers.

# We Care for the Things Around Us

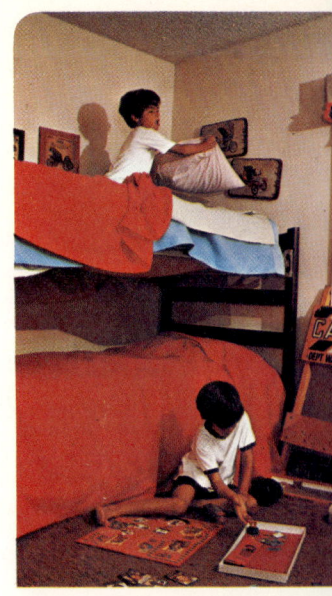

God gives us many good things.
But we must care for them.

Once, after Jesus fed many people,
  He said to His friends,
  "Pick up the bread
    that is left over.
  Do not let it go to waste."
Why do you think Jesus said that?

23

# Cities and Towns Are Wonderful

Do you live in a city or town?
Jesus did sometimes.
He loved His own city, Jerusalem.
He loved to walk in its streets
    and talk to people.
Jesus loved all the people
    in His city.

# We Enjoy the Country

Do you enjoy the country?
Do you like to walk in the woods?
Do you like to play on the grass?

Jesus also loved the country.
He liked to walk in the fields,
    talking to people.
He helped them with their troubles.

# We Enjoy the World God Gives Us

Do you like the sun,
    and the rain,
    and the wind?

The sun warms us.
The rain helps to make things grow.
The wind cools us.

Jesus also enjoyed the sun,
    and the rain,
    and the wind.
Jesus told us that they are gifts
    from God.

# 3. Jesus Helps People

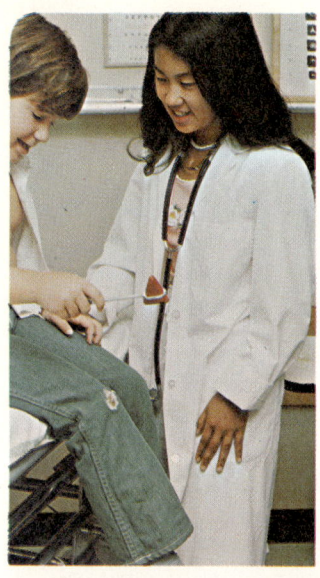
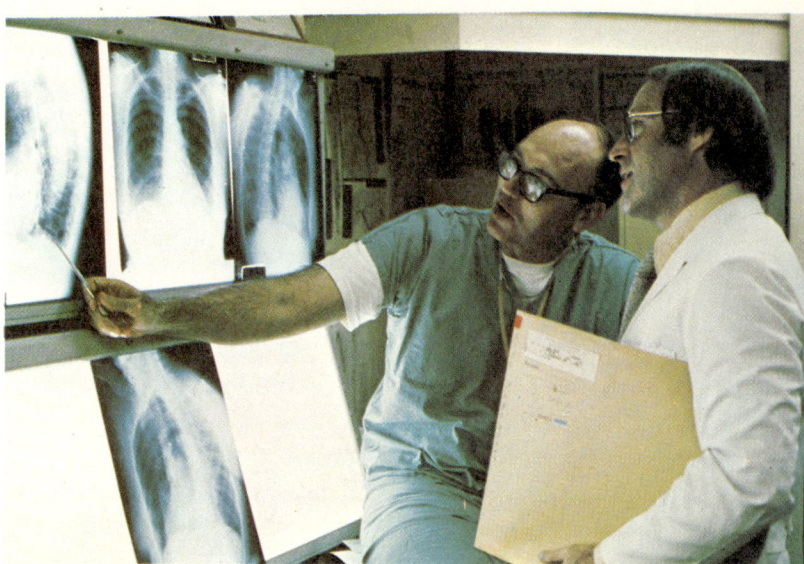
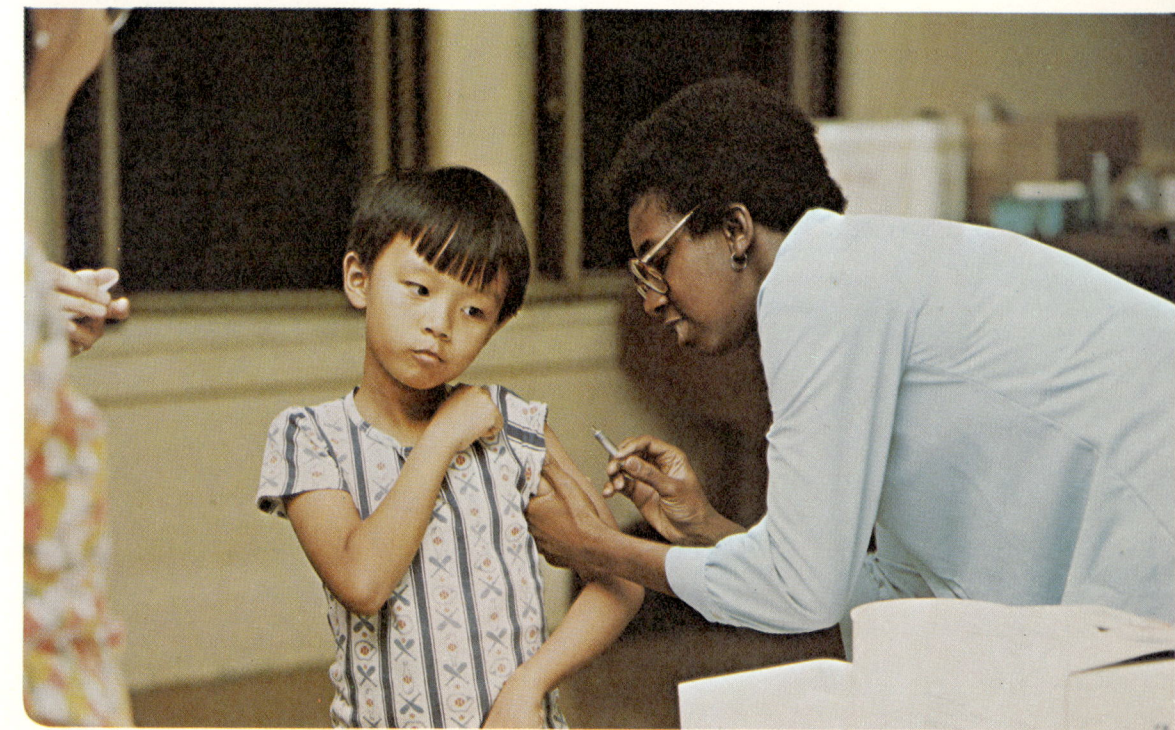

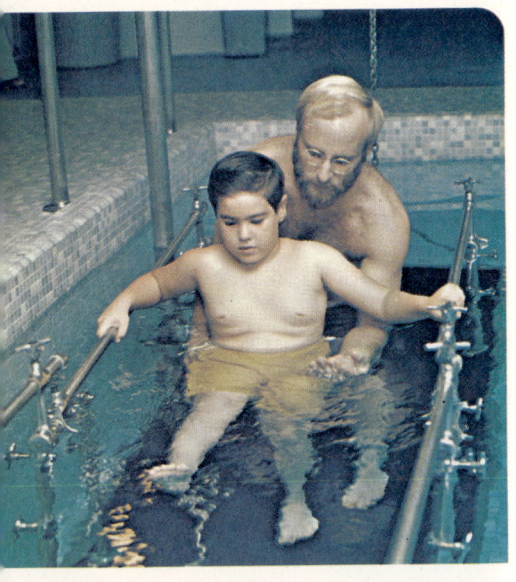

# Jesus Helps Sick People

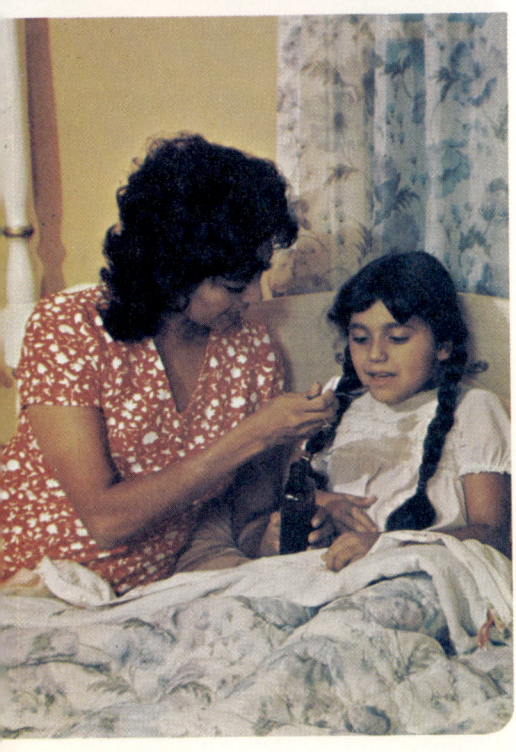

Jesus always wants to help people in need.
Once, a boy was very sick.
His father came to Jesus.
The father said, "Jesus, please help my little boy."

Jesus felt sorry for the poor, worried father.
He felt sorry for the sick boy.
Jesus said, "I will cure him."

The boy became well.
He was so happy.
The boy's father was happy, too.

# Jesus Helps People at Work

Jesus cares for working people.
Many of His friends were farmers
   and fishermen.

Once, some friends of Jesus
   were fishing.
But, they could not catch any fish.

Jesus knew how worried
   His friends were.
He knew that they needed the fish
   to sell for money.
So, Jesus showed His friends
   where to catch the fish.

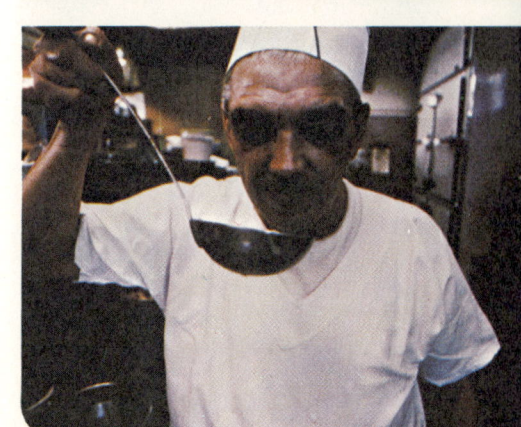

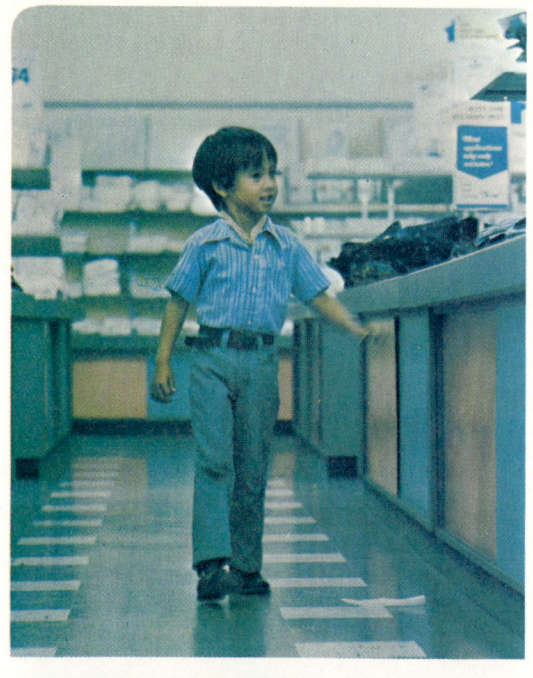

# Jesus Helps People Who Are Afraid

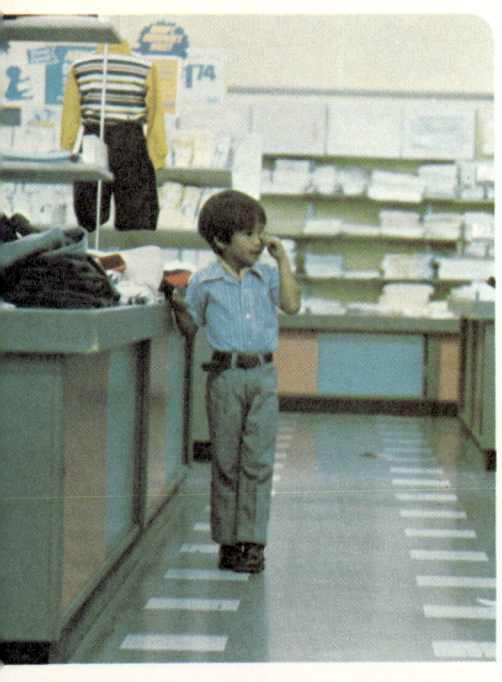

Jesus helps people who are afraid.
He helps people who are in trouble.

Once, some of His friends
    were sailing on a lake.
A storm came up.
The waves were high,
    and the wind was strong.
Jesus was with His friends.
But they were still afraid.

Jesus knew that His friends
    were afraid.
So, he calmed the storm for them.
How happy His friends were then!
Now they were not afraid!

# Jesus Helps Hungry People

Jesus does not want people
   to go hungry.
He wants people to have enough
   to eat.

One day, Jesus talked
   to a large crowd of people.
They were in the country,
   and it was getting late.
The people began to get hungry.
They had no food with them.

Jesus knew the people
   were hungry.
So He fed them with bread and fish.
The people were so happy.

"Jesus, please bless my food."

## Jesus Tells Us to Help People

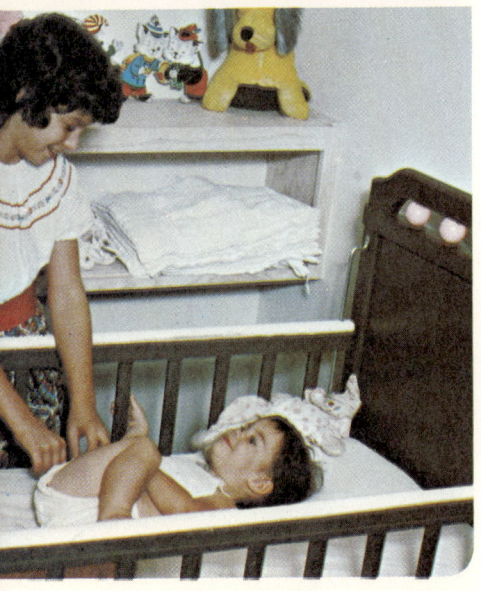

Jesus wants us to help people. He said to His friends,
> "Love one another as I have loved you."

This means that we are to love and help people in any way that we are able.

# THE MAN WHO LOVED HIS SHEEP

1. Once there was a good shepherd. He gave all his sheep pet names, and fed them well. He hugged them and tucked them in at night. He kept the wolves away.

2. We are not sheep. We are people. But Jesus cares for us the very same way.

## 4. Jesus Teaches Us About His Family

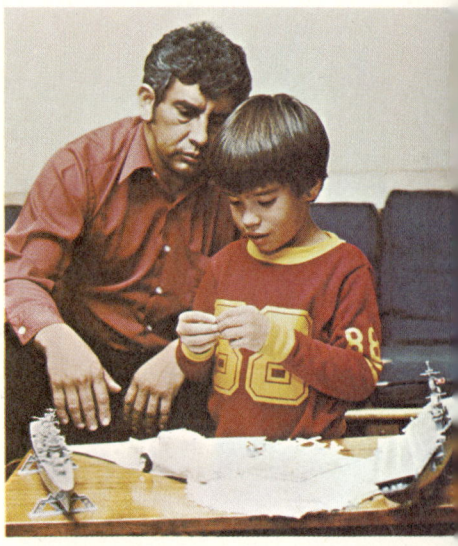

# Jesus Tells Us That God Is His Father

Jesus tells us that God
   is His Father.
He tells us that God is
   our Father, too.

Jesus loves His Father.
He shows us how to pray to Him.
Jesus tells us what to say:

"Our Father, who art in heaven,
   hallowed be Thy name;
Thy kingdom come;
Thy will be done on earth
   as it is in heaven.
Give us this day our daily bread;
and forgive us our trespasses
   as we forgive those
   who trespass against us;
and lead us not into temptation,
   but deliver us from evil.
Amen."

# Jesus Tells Us That God Our Father Always Loves Us

Jesus says that God our Father
   always loves us.
He says that God our Father
   always forgives us, too.

Knowing these things will help us
   to forgive people who hurt us.

Knowing that Jesus was kind
   to people will help us
   to be kind, too.

"Jesus, we will be kind like You.
We will help people
   when we are able.
Jesus, we want to please
   our Father."

# We Are All Members of God's Family

We are members of God's Family.
Jesus says that all people who
　　love His Father are His
　　brothers and sisters.

We become a special part
　　of God's Family at Baptism.
At Baptism, we become children
　　of God our Father.
We also become brothers
　　and sisters of Jesus.

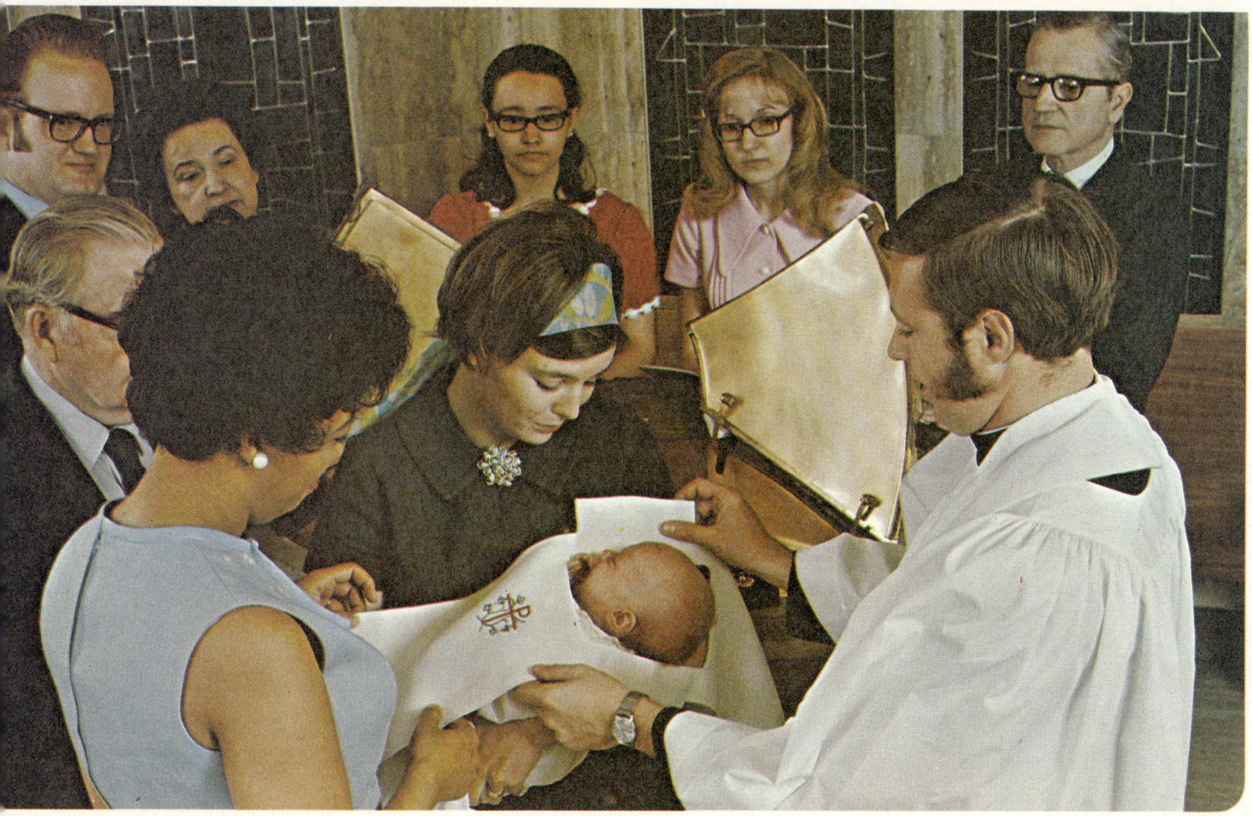

# Jesus Helps His Brothers and Sisters Today

Jesus helps His brothers and
    sisters today.
He gives us parents.
He helps parents to love
    each other and their children.
He helps them to care for
    the family and each other.

Jesus also gives us bishops
    and priests.
They help us to learn about Jesus
    and His Father.
They help us to pray together as
    the Family of God.

## The Family of God Gathers at Mass

We are the Family of God.
Each week, we go to Mass.
We pray to our Father at Mass.
We listen to God's words.
We remember what Jesus did
    at the Last Supper.

At Communion time, Jesus comes
    to us.
Jesus is our food.
He helps us to be kind to others.
He helps us to forgive people
    when they hurt us.

# We Act Like Jesus

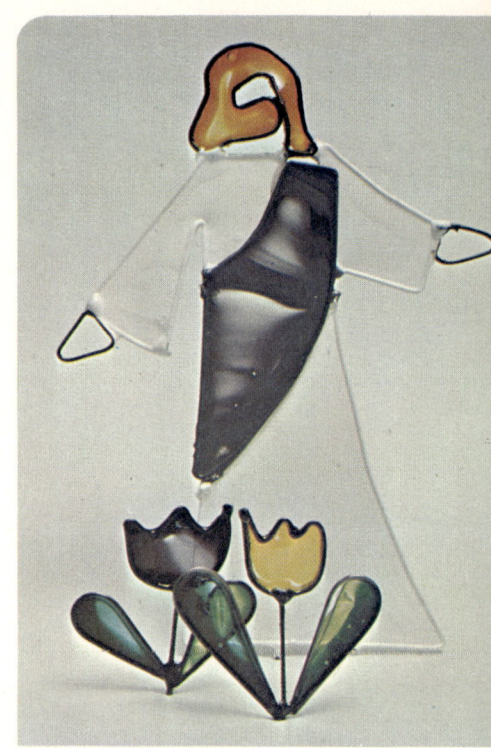

We do not see Jesus Himself today.
But we do see other people.
Jesus wants us to help people:
- to be nice to people,
- to love and obey our parents,
- to share our things.

Jesus wants us
- to study hard in school,
- to keep ourselves well.

"Jesus, we will love all people.
We will help them
   in every way that we can."

# The Life of Jesus

# Mary Is God's Mother and Our Mother, Too

God our Father wanted someone
 to be the Mother of Jesus.
He looked over the whole world.
God our Father chose Mary.
Mary is the holiest and best
 of all people.

God sent an angel to tell Mary
 the news.
The angel came to Mary and said,
 "Hail, Mary, full of grace.
 The Lord is with you."
These words mean,
 "Mary, you are holy.
 God loves you very much.
 He has chosen you."
Then the angel told Mary that she
 was to be the Mother of Jesus.

Mary was happy to hear the words
   of the angel.
She is happy to hear us say them, too.
We say these same words
   when we say Mary's prayer.

Mary went to visit her cousin,
   Elizabeth.
Elizabeth was happy that Mary
   was to be the Mother of Jesus.
Elizabeth said to Mary,
   "Blessed are you among women,
   and blessed is the fruit
   of your womb."
These words mean,
   "Mary, God has blessed you
   more than anyone in the world.
   And your baby will be Jesus,
   the holy One."
We say Elizabeth's words when
   we say Mary's prayer.

Jesus loves His Mother very much.
He loves us very much, too.
Jesus wants to share with us
    the best things He has.
So Jesus gave us Mary to be
    our Mother, too.
Mary loves us as her own children.
She cares for us just as she cared
    for Jesus.

We pray to Mary, our Mother.
We ask her to care for us.
We pray that someday we
    will be happy with Jesus
    and Mary in heaven.
We say,
    "Holy Mary, Mother of God,
    pray for us sinners, now,
    and at the hour of our death."

The "Hail Mary" is Mary's prayer.

# The First Christmas

It was late at night.
It was cold and dark.
Shepherds were sleeping
   in the fields, under the stars.

All of a sudden, the sky lit up.
The sky was full of angels.
They were singing a joyful song.
The angels spoke to the shepherds,
   "Jesus is born!
   Go to Bethlehem!
   You will find Him there
     in a stable!"

The shepherds ran to the stable.
There they found the baby Jesus.
He was sleeping in the arms
   of His mother, Mary.

Mary smiled at the shepherds.
Joseph, the foster father of Jesus, smiled, too.
It was the first Christmas day.
It was the birthday of Jesus.

# Jesus Grows Up

Jesus lived with Mary and Joseph
in a little town called Nazareth.

When Jesus was twelve years old,
Mary and Joseph took Him
on a long trip.
They went to the big city, Jerusalem.
In Jerusalem, Jesus, Mary, and
Joseph prayed in the Temple.

One day, Mary and Joseph
   could not find Jesus.
They looked everywhere for Him.
They found Him in the Temple.
Jesus was talking to the wise men.
He was telling them about God,
   His Father.

The wise men were listening to Jesus.
Mary and Joseph went up
   and hugged Jesus.
They were so happy to find Him.
Then Jesus went back home
   with His parents.

# Jesus Cares For People

When Jesus grew up, He went
   to other towns and cities.
Everywhere Jesus went, people
   came to see and to hear Him.
Some people came on crutches.
They were lame.
Jesus cured them.

Once, when Jesus walked by,
   a blind man called out to Him.
Jesus touched him.
The blind man was able
   to see again.

Everywhere Jesus went,
   He helped people.
He made them happy.
Jesus told the people,
   "Try to love each other
   the way I love you all."

# A Big Party

Once, Jesus and Mary and
   their friends were at
   a wedding party.
Everyone was happy.
There was plenty to eat.
But Mary saw something
   that no one else saw.
She saw that there would soon
   be no more wine.
Mary felt bad.
She knew that the party would
   be spoiled.
People would go home early.

So Mary went to Jesus.
She knew that Jesus would help
   if she asked Him.
And Jesus did help.
He changed water into wine
   because Mary asked Him to.

# Jesus Told Stories

Jesus spent a lot of time
    teaching the people.
The people wanted to know
    about God's love.

Jesus told the people about
    God's love.
He told them stories.
He told them stories about
    animals and plants,
    and parties and farms,
    and how parents love
        their children.
All these stories helped
    the people see how God,
    our Father, loves us all.

# Jesus Has a Special Meal

The night before He died,
  Jesus had a special meal
  with His best friends.
It is called the Last Supper.

First, Jesus told His friends,
  "Love one another
  as I have loved you."

Then He took bread in His hands.
He said, "This is my body."
Then Jesus took a cup of wine.
He said, "This is my blood."

Jesus gave His friends
    the holy Food to eat.
He said, "Do this in memory
    of me."

# Jesus Gives His Life for His Friends

That night, soldiers took Jesus.
They put Him in prison.
They did not believe that Jesus
 is the Son of God.

The next day, the soldiers nailed
 Jesus to a cross.
Jesus died and His friends
 buried Him in a tomb.

Jesus was brave.
He could have fought back.
But He did not fight back.
He would not lie, either.
He was God's Son!
Jesus was true to His Father.

## Jesus Is With Us

Mary Magdalene was a friend of Jesus.
Three days after Jesus died, Mary went to His tomb.
Mary found the tomb empty.
"Where is Jesus?" she thought.

Then, Mary saw a man.
The man spoke.
He was Jesus.
Jesus is alive!

That evening, Jesus came
    to His apostles.
He ate with them.
Thomas, one of the apostles,
    was not there.
Later, the apostles told Thomas
    that they saw Jesus.
But Thomas would not believe
    that Jesus was alive.
Thomas said,
    "Jesus is dead.
    He is not alive."

On another day, Jesus came again.
Thomas was there.
Jesus said, "Thomas, come here.
　　Look at me and touch me.
　　Now do you believe
　　　that I am alive?"
Thomas said, "My Lord and my
　　God!"
Jesus was alive.
He would never die again.

When the Holy Spirit came,
    He filled the friends of Jesus
        with joy.
He helped them to see clearly
    who Jesus is.

Now, the apostles knew
    what to do.
They began to tell all the people
    that Jesus is the Son of God!

"In the name of the Father,
    and of the Son,
    and of the Holy Spirit.
Amen."

# Prayers

**THE SIGN OF THE CROSS**

In the name of the Father,
   and of the Son,
   and of the Holy Spirit.
Amen.

**THE LORD'S PRAYER**

Our Father, who art in heaven,
   hallowed be Thy name;
Thy kingdom come;
Thy will be done on earth
   as it is in heaven.
Give us this day our daily bread;
and forgive us our trespasses
   as we forgive those
   who trespass against us;
and lead us not into temptation,
   but deliver us from evil.
Amen.

## THE HAIL MARY

Hail Mary, full of grace!
The Lord is with you;
blessed are you among women,
    and blessed is the fruit
      of your womb, Jesus.
Holy Mary, Mother of God,
    pray for us sinners, now,
    and at the hour of our death.
Amen.

## GLORY BE TO THE FATHER

Glory be to the Father,
    and to the Son,
    and to the Holy Spirit.
As it was in the beginning,
    is now, and always will be,
    forever and ever.
Amen.

**PRAYER BEFORE MEALS**

Dear Father,
    thank you for the food before me.
Thank you for all the growing things that I can eat.
Thank you, too, for making me your child.
Amen.

**PRAYER AFTER MEALS**

Dear Father,
    I have eaten the good things that You have given me.
May they help to give me strength to do your work today.
Amen.